The Light in Dark Places

The
Light
in
Dark Places

Matt Anderson

© Matt Anderson 2021

gatapoetry@gmail.com

ISBN 9798516800757

Edited and designed by Tell Tell Poetry

Printed in the United States of America

First Printing, 2021

For those who are struggling, have struggled, and will struggle. You are not alone because there is a God whose grace covers all things. There is hope in Jesus.

Contents

Acknowledgments

Thank you to my parents, Steve and Elizabeth Anderson, who have loved me, invested in my faith, and been a true example of what Christ looks like as a father and a mother.

To my brothers, Clay and Kyle Anderson, thank you for always loving me, supporting me, and keeping me grounded in the rock of Jesus. You are my best friends.

Finally, thank you to those around me, especially my family and close friends, who have loved me continuously and pointed me back to the cross. Without you all, I would not be the man I am today.

The Light in Dark Places

My Heart

Listen,
I don't like who I am, filled with this pain
But empty at the same time.
I just come into the room, try to clear my head
And fill it up with some clean rhymes.

But my life is a mess—who do I impress?
I'm waiting around for a new sign.
So, look back, but don't backtrack.
Don't get caught in my webs,
Spinning my life away on fine lines.

That's what it is, right?
A fine line
Like thin ice, I could break at any time.
A new sign? Like a billboard that shows who I am.
An old life,
A man who's dead inside.

I just want a quick fix
And I want my thoughts to quit.
I just want to be alive in my mind.

Letting go of things I'm attached to.
Time keeps ticking even when I'm in bad moods.
What's the cost of change?
Can I afford to pay my way through?

You don't know what love is
Until you're holding onto something you can't lose.
But here I am with nothing to hold onto.
Just writing these rhymes that look like my heart,
A dark room.

Alone

When you feel alone,
It's like you're running through the cold.
Feel the chill all the way to your bones.
I look around. Is anybody home?
I guess they left—they weren't ready to see my soul.

It's a place where I come and I stare—
A hole right through my life
Like the wind that courses through the air
But drifting somewhere. I'm scared.
I want to get lost in my dreams, but it's far from a dream.
    Nightmare.

Forgive me, these lines are dark.
I just have those days, the kind that steal the light.
A fire that wants to burn—pour some gas and watch it
    spark.
It's crazy, right? Look at me and you don't see the hurt.
But it's there. You don't look close enough—look inside my heart.

This is heavy, I know.
A street filled with questions, unknowns.
Hop in the car and let me pave this road.
I want to open up, but I don't want you to judge me—no.
Because my heart is broken.
Can't look inside my heart—it's stone.
Running through my thoughts. Shoot 'em up, Al Capone.
Remember this feeling? Alone.

Alone?
Yeah, it's me again—
Writing these rhymes,
Wrestling with my sin.

Hasn't been long, I know. How ya been?
I'm struggling. Where do I begin?
Do I let somebody in?
The game of life, how do I win?
Take a hammer, smash the pieces, put 'em back together,
    Amen?

Amen.

Dancing with the Devil

Come to me and I'll give you everything—
Everything you've ever wanted.
You search for more. I can give it to you.
Whatever it is, all are flaunted.

So enticing, you jump right in,
Not knowing what I have planned.
I come to steal, kill, and destroy;
Beat you down until you can't stand.

So dance with me.
Come dance with the devil.
I can give you what you desire.
Come dance with me. Let me spin you around . . .
Until you slowly drown in my fire.

The things of this world—
Affections so counterfeit and so sweet.
Oh child, so little do you know.
Everything I've been feeding you makes you weak.

But here you are, dancing with me,
Not a care in the world on your shoulders.
Because you have everything—everything you want and
   need—
Dancing here with the devil.

So dance with me.
Still dancing with the devil.
I've given you what you desire.
Come dance with me. I'll spin you around,
Slowly watching you burn in my fire.

Now that you're here, there's no need to pray.
No need to seek anything else.
The things of the world will prey on your faith.
You don't need that book on the shelf.

Those pages are empty words.
Come dance with me again. Remember the joys of today?
They can't give you what I have!
God can't save you. He left you, but I'm here to stay.

So let me play a song over you—
A song of the redeemed,
A lie to fill your head, the sin that leaves you dead,
A song leading straight back to me!

Dance with me, oh child.
I'll spin you around.
The devil beside you, let me see that smile.
And we'll continue to spiral down.

Let go of God because He let go—it's true.
Open your eyes,
Finally, to see that the only things you have
Are the lies I've been feeding you.

Where are you going?
The dance isn't over.
Come close and hear the chorus.
Let me draw you closer.

What?
Is it not what you wanted?
The desires of your heart, the things of the world.
This is what you told me, when we first started.

This dance isn't old,
It'll fill you, I promise!
Don't stray away from me.
He can't give you what I took in the Garden.

Father, this child is mine.
Look at her—broken, lost, heart stolen.
You don't want her. She's been dancing with sin.
Leave her, like you left me dancing away in my passion.

Forsake her like you forsook me.
Like you forsook your Son,
Remember him?
Hanging dead on the tree.

Alive in faith? She's dead, too.
What is it now?
You're feeding her garbage-truth?
Isn't that cute.

A heel to strike my head,
A snake being crushed,
An outcast from Heaven,
And I'll be the one left for dead!

Wait, your Son is alive?
I saw him dangling,
Smothered in blood,
The day the darkness covered Calvary.

A light is what you call him.
Yet I call it a dark dance
Because my slyness is so enticing,
She can't see where her death began.

You won't win this. No, not this time.
She's too far gone—
Can't reach her, can't have her.
Grace can't win, if I'm sublime.

So stop trying with her.
We all know who's to blame.
A loving Father removing his greatest warrior from Heaven.
So selfish—all you want is fame.

So I'll dance
And I'll spin her around.
She stands no chance with a Father like you
Saying you know what's best for a child.

What's this? A revelation?
A means to my own end?
Jesus is the way, the truth, and the life.
I've heard it all before, Father.
We will see who wins her in the end.

Get Behind Me

Here I am,
Going about my life and my plans.
No worry in the world,
No sand to sink in.

Stepping on the stones,
Reading the book, and praying fast.
I'm encouraged in my faith.
How long will my faith last?

The stairs lead up,
But you find ways to drag me down.
A man built on the rock,
But something cracking in the foundation.

Take shots at me—
That's what you're best at right?
When I start to find my way,
You lie to me, take my sight.

I'm done playing your games,
Reading into your lowly cries.
Fear is a liar
And I refuse to fear you this time.

Get behind me.
I'm done feeding on you.
You've taken enough of my life.
I'm holding onto the truth.

A snake,
Remember your name?
An angel, once righteous,
Now all you are is shame.

Once a problem,
A toil to struggle with.
But I recall what Jesus said
About crushing you in the end.

So, go on—
Give it all you've got.
I might stumble, fall, sin,
But I know Elohim, my God.

Living Again

Why do I get this way?
The lights shine on my face,
But I cower and run away—
Can't face my fears of today.

They swallow me up and spit me out like waves.
They sing to me of all my disgrace and it covers me.
Feeling so lost and helpless—no faith, no grace.

So separated from the world around me,
Like the wave as it reaches shore.
It crashes, so astounding
That people can look me in the eyes and they can't even find
    me.

But why should I expect them to find me?
I've searched all these years,
All the while, my sins are so binding,
Covering me in fear.

I guess, if I'm honest with myself,
It's the timing that eats me alive
Because I can be surrounded by those I love,
Yet feel so empty inside.

Let me try to explain this feeling,
So you can really understand what I'm meaning.
The hole inside my chest? That's a cave,
Overwhelmingly demeaning.

You should see what lives there—
A soul that's screaming, a heart that's bleeding,
A man crying inside for someone to help.
But the help won't come, so he stops believing.

You really know that place well
And it feels so dry—that well, empty, a shell.
Don't you see that's why this hole is so big?
Because people come and destroy you—a living hell.

So please don't leave me alone to myself.
That's when my thoughts flood my head.
I grab a raft and drift along to my own distress,
And wow . . . what a mess.

Cobwebs inside my heart,
Filling me slowly until the end.
So here I am—a man whose heart dug his grave,
Left him for dead.

But there You are, standing so close to me,
Even if I feel so far. . . .
You read me like a book.
You know when I'm upset, when I'm broken. You see my scars.

So You sit here, just sit until the hurting stops.
I've been praying for You for a long time.
Honestly thought my prayers were lost—
Obviously not.

Because here You are,
Reminding me that I'm loved by the One who created the stars.
And You love me just the same,
Even when I'm lost in my thoughts.

I would never have seen this coming and we've come so far.
Although there's a hole in my heart,
I can slowly feel it being filled
By the love that You are.

Slowly sanctify with me
And let's move through the pain.
And one day, we can look back,
Look upon that place.

The place where love filled our hearts
And took away the sting, so to say.
Death has been defeated
And I'll sing Your praises all of my days.

Idols

Idols might grab my attention,
But You're in a different dimension.
While my eyes were fixed on idols,
It was Your Son who made the dissension.

A ransom for people like me,
Who look to the world to fill our needs.
A blind man who can't see—
It's not the idols, but Jesus, who sets us free.

Our idols are simply chains,
Suffocating our dead hearts.
Maybe it's fear to blame?
You're afraid to let go, comfortable,
But comfortable is full of shame.

Take that first leap—
A leap of faith,
A cry for God,
A thirst for His never-ending Grace.

He gives it with no end,
Free of the chains.
A chain-breaker indeed,
In Jesus's name.

The Godman who rose from the dead—
A body like ours, broken as bread.
Call on Him and His everlasting love.
He'll take your idols, turn them into dust.

Spirit Be Near

Waking up on the wrong side of the bed,
Not who I want to wake up as.
Someone I'm familiar with,
But not the one I want to fill my head.

I wake up knowing who I am,
The person empty inside.
Headspace funny, full of nothing-fuzz,
Fully aware, I open my eyes.

I get up and move.
My feet hit the floor with no dance.
I want so badly to feel Your Grace.
Touch my heart, Lord. Let me feel Your hands.

So, I go and take care of me,
Doing what I need to do.
Yet, I haven't really woken up
Because I neglect the time I need with You.

Here I am—
Physically awake, spiritually asleep.
And I know how I am feeling—
Dead to You and alive to me.

Come home after my work,
Walk into a study in my living room.
Feeling separated from it all,
What I yearn for is Your presence, a change of mood.

I fall on my knees, face buried in my bed.
My thoughts, scattered prayers.
Can You hear me, Lord?
Or, just like my spirit, are these words dead?

God, why do I feel this way?
Selfish ambitions and thoughts of mine.
Please, oh Lord, crush my iniquities,
So my heart and life can reflect thine.

You enter the room,
While my thoughts and prayers run wild.
Sitting quietly, being still with me,
Hearing my silence fill the air, all the while.

God, I stretch out my hands.
I need to feel Your healing touch.
Please, make Yourself known to a beggar.
It's Your omnipresence I long for so much.

And a song plays in the background,
Softly screaming over my prayers to You.
A man with his knees on the floor,
Thirsting for God and playing this tune.

God, You know where I've been.
You were there with me then.
You were faithful before.
You'll be faithful again.
I'm holding Your hand.

And as the lyrics pour out,
With the overwhelming silence so loud,
There is a hand that touches mine—
The Spirit of Yours whom You used to reach down.

His cup concomitantly full,
Because of Your Grace that abounds.
It was You, Jesus, reaching for me,
Making known that Your Love is profound.

Perspective

Scratch the surface and you'll see
A man who struggles with nothing, it seems.

Someone who has it figured out,
A man who fits in with the crowd.

A sturdy soul—consistent, foolproof.
A man who looks the part, wearing his costume.

Struts the walk and talks the talk.
A man whose life is full and his cup is tall.

A smile stretches across his face—
Full to the brim with hope and grace.

I've performed this act for years.
It's second nature now, or so it appears.

Suppress the things that are true.
I do this well—fooled both myself and you.

My life is an ocean, deep and wide.
You say you know me, but haven't seen what's inside.

It's only on the surface, can't you see?
This reflection screams lies of who I claim to be.

It's purely perspective, that's all it is.
Yet I've fooled a lot of people, me included.

I've got it all together, yet I'm broken inside.
A puzzle with so many pieces—different struggles and lies.

Continually searching for answers in life,
Maybe finding them means to humble myself and lay down
    my pride.

But who am I to say?
I have this life-thing figured out; I've fooled us anyway.

Diving deeper is not the answer for you.
My life is heavy. Underneath the waves, you'd find truth.

And truth, they say, sets you free.
But it's the truth I'm scared of—the real me.

So, turn away. Please turn your head,
That I may live in freedom from the man within.

Pruning, I've had a lot of that—
Scars here and there, memories of my past.

A dark place, a heart that's been lost.
A man beaten, broken, like the man on the cross.

Yet it was Him who looked at me in the now—
Saw me where I was, while blood poured from His brow.

The thorns He wore were the sins I swore.
But He looked on me with grace, even while broken and torn.

Never really seeing His perspective,
Jesus saw me worth dying for, even when I was reckless.

Now truly, truly, I say to you,
I'm not the man I once was and His scars are the proof.

My life, heavy indeed.
Still don't have it figured out, but there's peace on my knees.

While I had myself and you fooled too,
The one man I couldn't fool was the beloved bridegroom.

His love an ocean, deep and wide,
A man found himself when he let Him inside.

Once searching for answers with nothing to find,
I say now with a full heart, it is love that won this time.

My sturdy soul—once a lie, now true—
Only because the Father sent His Son for me and you.

I guess they were right—truth does set you free—
Because I know that truth was bound to that faithful tree.

An act performed purely out of love
Was the Grace of God—Jesus, His Son—Heaven-sent from above.

Now my perspective, forever changed.
Thank you, Lord, for seeing me and remembering my name.

Diamonds

Sand, what man was made from.
Something from the ground,
Something low, something rough.
Like the life we live—simple, but complicated enough.

Feel it slip right through your hands,
The life we live.
Simple yet complicated.
Gone—we blink and it ends.

The pressures of the world
Laying heavy on our souls.
Looking around,
Searching for that forever gold.

That forever gold,
What is it?
A feeling of belonging, love, purpose?
Or a heart full of emptiness?

Yet we look past the pressure—
Past the hurt, the pain, the trials.
And here we are, so oblivious
That it's the pressure in the sand that creates the diamonds.

The Gates

When I'm worn down to nothing,
The world around me buzzing,
The noise is so loud, it's hard to focus.
Keep Your distance. Soul diminished. Please don't judge me.

Because I'm fighting with myself,
But there's a book that sits on my shelf.
Maybe if I opened it up, it would help me escape my own hell.
It's like a bell—ring it once, I'm at the door.
You here to help?
Because that's what we all need, right?
Help.

You reach out, but it scares me.
It's not who You are, but who I can be.
I run so far—like an ocean in front of us, the end we can't see.
So, I dive and You preach—*hold on to me*—but I know my
   heart is chest-deep.
A heart that can be cold, facing my problems. The water
   over my head now,
Drowning.

Are these pages even turning?
My thoughts are heavy, my heart is yearning.
But when I feel alone, it's like everyone deserts me.
On the floor, it feels like doors are shutting.
Jesus, give me the strength and faith to keep fighting.
When I'm down to nothing, I need my faith to restore my
   searching.
I need Your water, or I'll be forever thirsting.
Quench my soul and show me Your love. Show me the
   reason for my hurting.

Pull me out of this place,
Set my soul ablaze.
I know You're in control.
So I'll trust that, in my hurting, it'll all be okay.
The sting of it all, not something that just goes away.
Remember when You said life is a flower? Slowly fades?
So let this slowly fade,
So I can wash myself in Your Grace that's new, every day.
So I can get up each morning and run this race.
So one day, I can see You face-to-face.
And on that day, You'll say,
Well done, my good and faithful servant. Open up the gate.

Move Me

I sit and watch,
But what am I doing?
Sitting and watching.
Shouldn't I be moving?
I put it off, looking for someone else to do it.

What if we all did that?
Would anything happen?
What if Jesus did that?
Then we wouldn't be laughing.

We can't save ourselves.
We're helpless and lost.
But I find myself, when I look at the cross.

What He did for me, I can't repay.
So I wake up thankful for life each day.

But why do I sit here?
Why am I without motion?
Lord, make me like a child,
My faith as deep as the oceans.

Make my life Your canvas.
I want people to see
How You came down and rescued me.

Give me a voice to speak what's right and true.
Give me a heart to seek nothing but You.
Give me feet to follow where You want me to go.
Give me strength to know You're in control.

Jesus, move in me.
Move so much that I can't be still.
Overflow my heart,
Lord, I want it to spill.

I don't want to sit here
And be stagnant in my faith.
I want to run and not grow weary.
I want to finish the race.

You deserve my everything.
I will give You my best.
I will praise Your name.
The gospel will not be laid to rest.

Make me move, oh Lord,
As far as the sky is wide.
Fill me with courage,
Knowing You're by my side.

Let me reach the ends of the Earth,
Knowing my work isn't done
Until the people around the world
Know the Father, Spirit, and Son.

AO1

The pressure is on.
The lights rain down.
All over the world,
People search for a crown,

A pedestal,
A place to sit—
That's what we think
Fills the hole within.

Don't make that mistake.
Don't live for yourself.
Because I promise you,
It's emptiness in itself.

Give up your seat,
Play the background,
Give up the controls—
It's God's time now.

His Grace is enough.
He gave you a platform.
So live for God—
Go against the norm.

Point all glory to Him
Because He is King.
He deserves our best.
So we'll keep living,

Not for ourselves,
But for the Lord above.
Through our platforms,
We can show Christ's love.

So glorify God.
He gave us His Son.
Let us bring praise to Him,
Living for an audience of One.

A Promise

For those who struggle to find a home—
You feel like you've taken your last step and there's no
    freeing the chains of being alone.

For those who feel the hole inside their chest—
An overwhelming sense of nothing that drives you to the edge.

For those who are fighting for something, but can barely
    hold on—
Your grip is weary and the strength you once had is frivolous
    and gone.

There's a home that I know all too well—
A place where orphans come to celebrate and angels sing
    praises to God Himself.

There's a love that takes the emptiness to the tomb
Because the love that hung on the tree is the light that
    overwhelms the darkness inside of you.

There's a love so strong that He was placed in the ground
And rose again the third day. There's no fight to win—
    only a crown.

So come to the cross, with all your burdens in hand,
And find yourself on your knees because that's where you'll
    finally stand.

The weight of this world is prefaced by a curse,
But the one who walked on the waters calms the storm when
    you feel submersed.

All the crying, the hurt, and the pain
Were put to death when his body was beaten, torn, and
blood-stained.

So in those moments when your tribulation seems never-ending,
Remember Jesus because He remembered you and promised
a new beginning.

The Best Is Yet to Come

We're living in desperate times.
But for now, we live our lives.
Just trying to pass it by,
Filling voids inside with different lies.

It's heavy, right?
A life that feels so long is quickly passing—bye.
The time we get, so full of emotion,
But gone in the blink of an eye.

So, don't blink—
This time doesn't stop moving.
It's a ticket you bought,
A showing of your own movie.

The screen is full of lessons, compromise, and losing.
Turn the page—life is a book.
Pick up a pen and script it.
The ink is pouring out, oozing.

Pay attention and don't skip a beat.
There're places you need to go, things to see, people to meet.
Eyes open, watching carefully.
This life is a journey, a puzzle—
Watch the pieces fill the scenes.

Each piece taking its place,
A picture forming, the artist brushes the page.
Each stroke is something new.
Is there peace? Only time will tell. Watch the picture that
    blooms.

There's hope in knowing there's another side,
A place where our lives are counted and prized.
The gift of Grace that covers us in red, wine.
The savior Jesus said, *Tetelestai*.

A battle forever won.
A life lived under our burning sun.
Separated no more because of the One.
I can say, with confidence,
The best is yet to come.

Made in the USA
Columbia, SC
25 June 2021